FRACTIONS AND DECIMALS FOR DUMMIES MATH ESSENTIALS
Children's Fraction Books

PROFESSOR GUSTO
EDUCATIONAL & INFORMATIVE BOOKS FOR CHILDREN
(PRE-K / K-12)

A fraction represents a part of a whole or, more generally, any number of equal parts.

A decimal number refers to any number written in decimal notation.

IDENTIFYING FRACTIONS - USING BLOCKS

Color the Fraction.

1. $\dfrac{1}{3}$ = ▯▯▯

2. $\dfrac{1}{2}$ = ▯▯

3. $\dfrac{2}{6}$ = ▯▯▯▯▯▯

4. $\dfrac{4}{10}$ =

5. $\dfrac{2}{5}$ =

6. $\dfrac{6}{8}$ =

7. $\dfrac{1}{5}$ =

8. $\dfrac{3}{6}$ =

9. $\dfrac{6}{10}$ =

10. $\dfrac{2}{3}$ =

11. $\dfrac{2}{4}$ =

12. $\dfrac{1}{8}$ =

13. $\dfrac{4}{6}$ = ⬚⬚⬚⬚⬚⬚

14. $\dfrac{2}{10}$ = ⬚⬚⬚⬚⬚⬚⬚⬚⬚⬚

15. $\dfrac{4}{5}$ = ⬚⬚⬚⬚⬚

16. $\dfrac{1}{4}$ =

17. $\dfrac{1}{10}$ =

18. $\dfrac{7}{10}$ =

19. $\dfrac{3}{8}$ =

20. $\dfrac{5}{6}$ =

21. $\dfrac{5}{8}$ =

IDENTIFYING FRACTIONS - USING BLOCKS

Write the Fraction.

1. 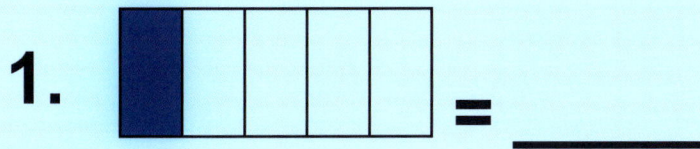 = _____

2. 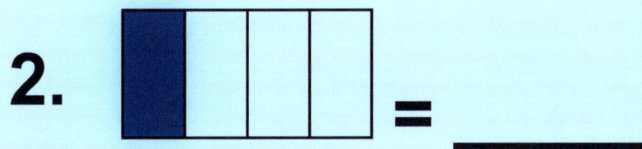 = _____

3. 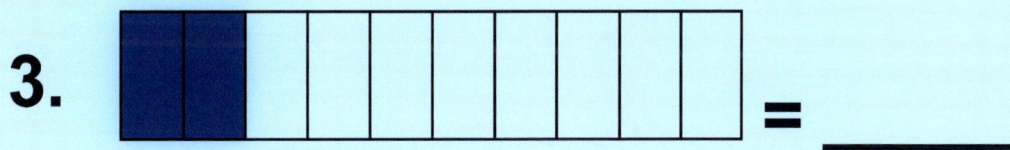 = _____

4. 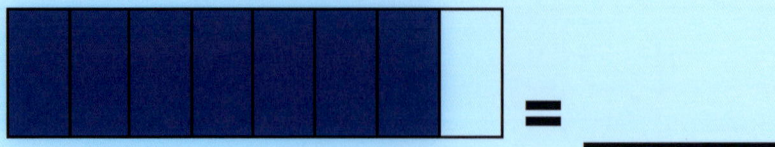 = _____

5. 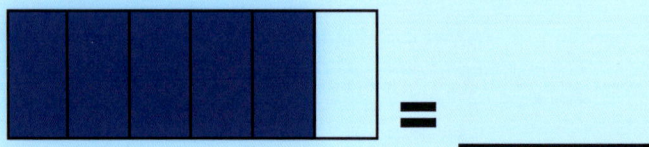 = _____

6. 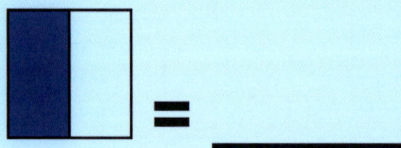 = _____

7. 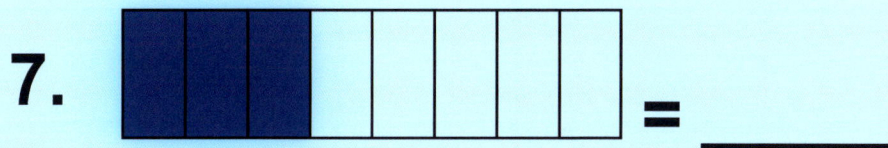 = _____

8. 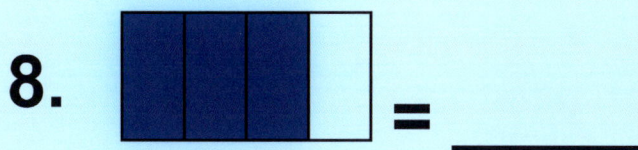 = _____

9. 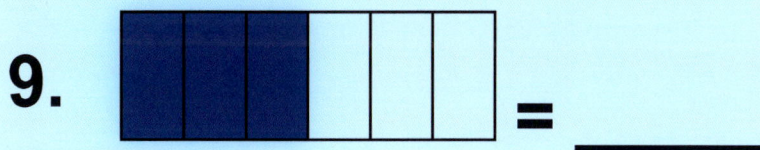 = _____

10. 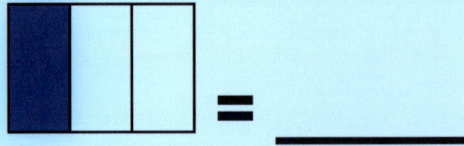 = _____

11. 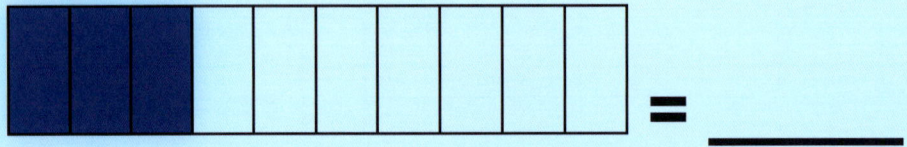 = _____

12.  = _____

13. 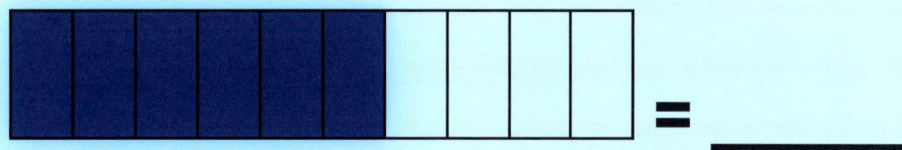 = _____

14. 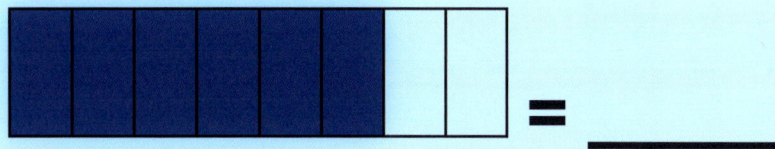 = _____

15. 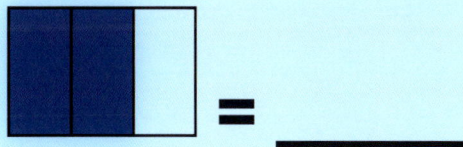 = _____

16. 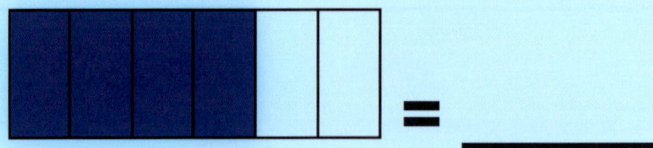 = _____

17. 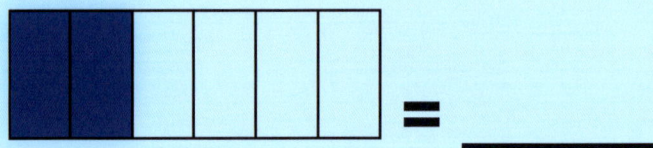 = _____

18. 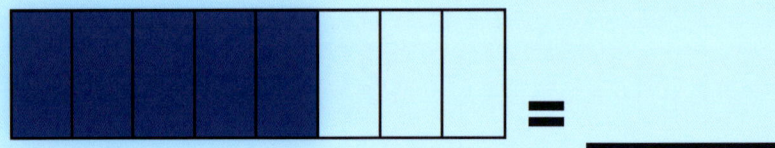 = _____

19. 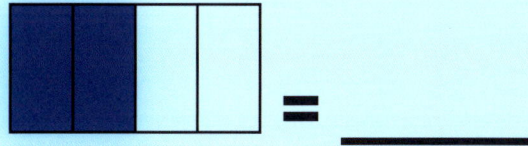 = _____

20. 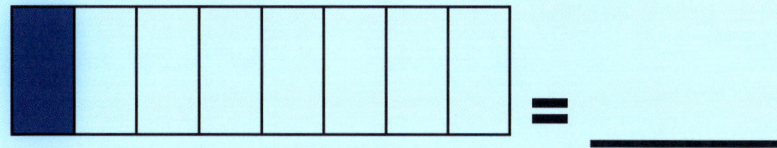 = _____

21. 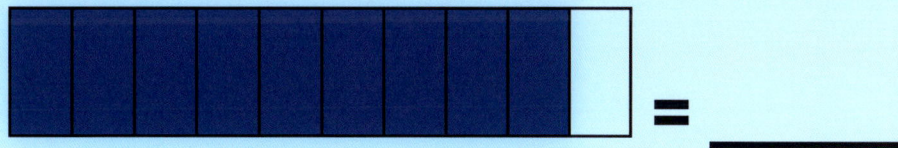 = _____

FRACTIONS TO DECIMALS

Convert the decimal.

1. $\dfrac{1}{2}$ = _____

2. $\dfrac{3}{4}$ = _____

3. $\dfrac{1}{10}$ = _____

4. $\dfrac{1}{5}$ = _____

5. $\dfrac{2}{8}$ = _____

6. $\dfrac{2}{10}$ = _____

7. $\dfrac{1}{4}$ = _____

8. $\dfrac{3}{10}$ = _____

9. $\dfrac{4}{8}$ = _____

10. $\dfrac{9}{10}$ = _____

11. $\dfrac{6}{8}$ = _____

12. $\dfrac{6}{10}$ = _____

13. $\dfrac{4}{10}$ = _____

14. $\dfrac{3}{6}$ = _____

15. $\dfrac{5}{10}$ = _____

16. $\dfrac{2}{4}$ = _____

17. $\dfrac{7}{10}$ = _____

18. $\dfrac{2}{5}$ = _____

19. $\dfrac{8}{10}$ = _____

20. $\dfrac{4}{5}$ = _____

21. $\dfrac{5}{20}$ = _____

MIXED NUMBERS TO DECIMALS

Convert the decimal.

1. $5\dfrac{6}{10}$ = _____

2. $4\dfrac{4}{10}$ = _____

3. $4\dfrac{9}{10}$ = _____

4. $6 \dfrac{1}{10}$ = _____

5. $3 \dfrac{2}{10}$ = _____

6. $2 \dfrac{8}{10}$ = _____

7. $2\dfrac{5}{10} =$ _____

8. $7\dfrac{6}{10} =$ _____

9. $5\dfrac{9}{10} =$ _____

10. $9\dfrac{5}{10}$ = _____

11. $1\dfrac{7}{10}$ = _____

12. $2\dfrac{2}{10}$ = _____

13. $3\dfrac{8}{10} =$ _____

14. $9\dfrac{1}{10} =$ _____

15. $2\dfrac{1}{10} =$ _____

16. $1\dfrac{1}{10} =$ _____

17. $7\dfrac{9}{10} =$ _____

18. $8\dfrac{5}{10} =$ _____

19. $1\dfrac{6}{10}$ = _____

20. $7\dfrac{7}{10}$ = _____

21. $9\dfrac{2}{10}$ = _____

ANSWER

1.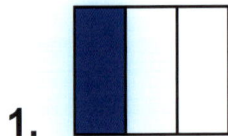

2.

3.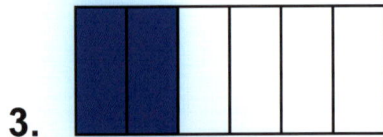

4.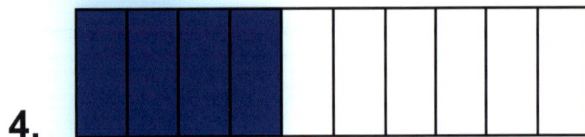

5.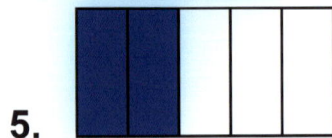

6.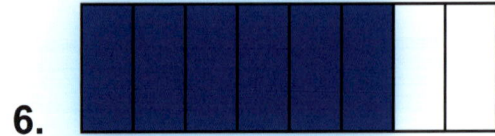

7.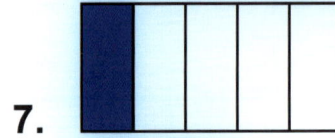

8.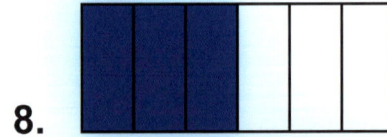

9.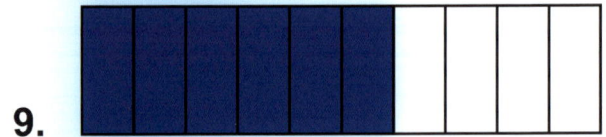

10.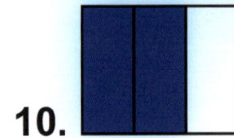

ANSWER

11.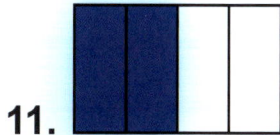

12.

13.

14.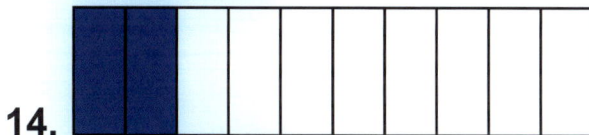

15.

16.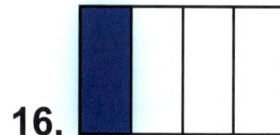

17.

18.

19.

20.

21.

ANSWER

1. $\dfrac{1}{5}$

2. $\dfrac{1}{4}$

3. $\dfrac{2}{10}$

4. $\dfrac{7}{8}$

5. $\dfrac{5}{6}$

6. $\dfrac{1}{2}$

7. $\dfrac{3}{8}$

8. $\dfrac{3}{4}$

9. $\dfrac{3}{6}$

10. $\dfrac{1}{3}$

11. $\dfrac{3}{10}$

12. $\dfrac{4}{5}$

13. $\dfrac{6}{10}$

14. $\dfrac{6}{8}$

15. $\dfrac{2}{3}$

16. $\dfrac{4}{6}$

17. $\dfrac{2}{6}$

18. $\dfrac{5}{8}$

19. $\dfrac{2}{4}$

20. $\dfrac{1}{8}$

21. $\dfrac{9}{10}$

ANSWER

1.	.5	12.	.6	1.	5.6	12.	2.2
2.	.75	13.	.4	2.	4.4	13.	3.8
3.	.1	14.	.5	3.	4.9	14.	9.1
4.	.2	15.	.5	4.	6.1	15.	2.1
5.	.25	16.	.5	5.	3.2	16.	1.1
6.	.2	17.	.7	6.	2.8	17.	7.9
7.	.25	18.	.4	7.	2.5	18.	8.5
8.	.3	19.	.8	8.	7.6	19.	1.6
9.	.5	20.	.8	9.	5.9	20.	7.7
10.	.9	21.	.25	10.	9.5	21.	9.2
11.	.75			11.	1.7		

Printed in Great Britain
by Amazon